I always get my sin

... at Ho* class ?

Beste Kathleen,
veel plezier
and good luck,

D1662725

Heerlen 31-8-2015

* = "two tongues only"

Maarten H. Rijkens

I ALWAYS GET MY SIN

Het bizarre Engels van Nederlanders

2015 Prometheus Amsterdam

Eerste druk 2005
Vijftigste druk 2015

De eerste negenendertig drukken verschenen bij uitgeverij BZZTÔH te
's-Gravenhage.

© Maheri Scriverius BV, Baarn
Ontwerp omslag: WIM Ontwerpers
Illustratie omslag: Kirsten Quast
Zetwerk: Elgraphic bv, Vlaardingen
www.uitgeverijprometheus.nl
ISBN 978 90 446 1505 0

CONTENT

Before word 7

Acknowledgments 11

1   Mutual introductions and social talk 15

2   Before starting the meeting 25

3   The meeting starts 33

4   General statements 41

5   The meeting is progressing 51

6   Things are not going well 59

7   Time-out 69

8   Things are going well 77

9   Agreement and signage of contract 85

10   Farewell dinner 93

'The Chaos', or 'a Dutchman's difficulties with the English language', by dr. Gerard Nolst Trenité (1870-1946)   103

Proposal for a more user-friendly English   115

Afterword 121

About the writer 127

BEFORE WORD

During 32 years I was employed by Heineken, for many years responsible for the Asia Pacific. During most of those years I either travelled fifty percent of my time or lived and worked in the outside country.

In that capacity I had many colleagues and met many friendly business associates, whose English was not always up to scratch. Dutch hotemetotes would make speeches and visiting ministers would address groups in hilarious ways. In Singapore I heard:'I am the first woman State Secretary for the Inside and I am having my first period.' A Dutch ex-parliamentarian said:'Previously, I was sitting in the Second Room.'

On 14 April 1988 a member of our Executive
Board was on his first visit to our company in
Singapore. During a dinner in the Gardenia
Room of the Shangri-La Hotel he said: 'Although
I do not have the grey hair of my predecessor
and although I do not speak such good English, I
always get my sin.' One of the Singapore
directors of our partner company looked at me
in total bewilderment and whispered: 'I always
get my sin?' Of course, I thought: it is me what, as
I sat completely with my mouth full of teeth.

Ever since that day I have carried with me a little
blocnote to jot down the interesting English
spoken by Dutch people, which I call 'Denglish'.
This quickly helped me on road. So this is not

just wet finger work, but an actual washing list of what I heard. 'How do you do and how do you do your wife?' has become my favourite, not to forget 'I thank you from the bottom of my heart and also from my wife's bottom.'

In this book the content speaks volumes. To print all of it was not to do, so this is not an exhausted list. But now that it has come from the ground, I clearly don't did this for nothing. I believe we should all be interesting in this subject and hopely you will enjoy it just as much as I do. Please deal it out on some friendly undertakers, because it is clear that it can so not longer.

Maarten H. Rijkens – Baarn, half 2005

ACKNOWLEDGMENTS

I worked myself the blubbers once I bit myself fast in all the Denglish I heard. And although I know precise who said what, where and when, I have decided not to indicate the source, as it may be embarrassing to many of those hotemetotes and could also be considered unsporty.

My father Rein Rijkens (1913-2003) and my mother Clara Wilhelmina Rijkens-Schrijver (1914-2003) always laughed their head off when I told them about certain Denglish remarks and they encouraged me to write this book. My father even made me aware of the poem 'The Chaos' by Dr. Gerard Nolst Trenité, which I have attached.

I, therefore, dedicate this book to them, with fond memories.

Maarten H. Rijkens

1

MUTUAL
INTRODUCTIONS
AND SOCIAL TALK

When the hotemetotes have just arrived, they first have to make introductions and do some social talk. They ask what do you, how do you do and how do you do your wife. Some are not the first the best and are working hardly. Some are doing easy these days.

HOW DO YOU DO AND HOW DO YOU DO YOUR WIFE?

Hoe gaat het met u en hoe gaat het met uw vrouw?

THANK YOU FOR YOUR RECENT WRITINGS

Dank voor uw recente schrijven

THERE ARE A LOT OF HOTEMETOTES!

Er zijn een heleboel hotemetoten!

WHAT DO YOU?

Wat doe je?

I AM THE FIRST WOMAN STATE SECRETARY FOR THE INSIDE...

Ik ben de eerste vrouwelijke staatssecretaris van Binnenlandse Zaken...

... AND I AM HAVING MY FIRST PERIOD

... en ik ben in m'n eerste ambtstermijn

I COULD NOT FIND THE HEAD ENTRANCE

Ik kon de hoofdingang niet vinden

DURING THE EARTHQUAKE THE BUILDING WAS SHAKING ON ITS FUNDAMENTALS

Tijdens de aardbeving stond het gebouw te schudden op z'n grondvesten

WHEN WAS THE REMOVAL OF MR. JANSEN TO LONDON?

Wanneer is de heer Jansen naar Londen verhuisd?

MY FAMILY AND I LIVED MANY YEARS IN THE OUTSIDE WORLD

Mijn familie en ik woonden vele jaren in het buitenland

I LIVED IN GERMANY DURING MY YOUNG YEARS

Ik woonde in Duitsland gedurende mijn jonge jaren

I NOW LIVE IN OLD SOUTH

Ik leef nu in Oud Zuid

INDEED, THIS IS MY SEAL RING WITH MY FAMILY WEAPON

Ja, dit is mijn zegelring met mijn familiewapen

I WAS A CAVALERY OFFICER BY THE HUSSARS OF BOREEL

Ik was een cavalerieofficier bij de huzaren van Boreel

IN THE BEGINNING TIME WE WERE JUST A SMALL COMPANY

In de begintijd waren we slechts een klein bedrijf

YOU DID MORE FOR THE COMPANY IN THE PAST THAN WE DID IN THE RECENT FUTURE

U heeft in het verleden meer voor de onderneming gedaan dan wij zelf in het recente verleden

WHAT DO YOU DO?

Wat voert u voor 'n beroep uit?

I FOCK HORSES

Ik fok paarden

PARDON?

Ja, paarden!

SHE WORKED HARDLY

Ze heeft hard gewerkt

I HAVE RECENTLY GONE WITH PENSION

Ik ben recentelijk gepensioneerd

I WAS VERY FOCUSSED ON MY FUCK

Ik was erg gefocussed op m'n vak

I EARNED MY SPURS IN ASIA AND NOW IT IS DIFFICULT TO LET IT LOOSE

Ik heb m'n sporen in Azie verdiend en nu is het moeilijk om het los te laten

BUT NOW I AM DOING EASY

Maar nu doe ik het rustig aan

PREVIOUSLY, I WAS SITTING IN THE SECOND ROOM

Voorheen zat ik in de Tweede Kamer

SHE IS NOT THE FIRST THE BEST

Zij is niet de eerste de beste

2

BEFORE
STARTING THE
MEETING

Before the meeting starts, it has to be decided by which points one has to stand still, what would be interested to know and in which matter clearing has to be found. Some guests are too late, some cannot attend because they are on rice and some are under way.

WHY IS HE TOO LATE?

Waarom is hij te laat?

HE HAD IT NOT STANDING IN HIS DIARRHOEA

Hij had het niet in z'n agenda staan

BUT HE IS UNDER WAY

Maar hij is onderweg

OVER THREE DAYS YOU CAN FLY BACK TO SINGAPORE OVER LONDON

Over drie dagen kunt u over Londen terug naar Singapore vliegen

YOUR PLANE LEAVES STIPTLY AT TEN FOR HALF TWO

Uw vliegtuig vertrekt stipt om tien voor half twee

I DID WENT THERE BEFORE

Ik ben daar eerder geweest

WHY IS MR. RIJKENS ON RICE?

Waarom is de heer Rijkens op reis?

BECAUSE THEY HAVE SOME FEASTDAYS IN HOLLAND

Omdat ze een paar feestdagen hebben in Holland

WE SHOULD ALL BE INTERESTING IN THIS SUBJECT

We zouden allemaal geïnteresseerd moeten zijn in dit onderwerp

BUT SOME PEOPLE ARE NOT INTERESTING

Maar sommige mensen zijn niet geïnteresseerd

WE ARE THERE BUSY WITH

We zijn er druk mee bezig

THE WORK PRESSION IS HIGH

De werkdruk is hoog

I WOULD LIKE TO STAND STILL BY THIS POINT

Ik zou bij dit punt willen stilstaan

WHAT WOULD BE INTERESTED TO KNOW?

Wat zou interessant zijn om te weten?

THIS IS NOT AN EXHAUSTED LIST

Dit is niet een uitputtende lijst

THEY HAVE IT ALL
Ze hebben 't al

I WILL SHOW THEM THE BACK OF MY TONGUE
Ik zal ze het achterste van m'n tong laten zien

LET ME BRING MORE CLEARING IN THE MATTER
Laat mij meer helderheid in de zaak brengen

I UNDERSTAND PRECISE WHAT YOU MEAN
Ik begrijp precies wat u bedoelt

WHAT FOR PEOPLE DO YOU NEED?

Wat voor mensen heb je nodig?

WE STILL HAVE TO SUCK
ONE LID

We moeten nog een lid zoeken

HE IS STILL NOT HERE, BUT HE IS ALREADY
ON ROAD

Hij is hier nog steeds niet, maar hij is al op weg

AM I SITTING FOR YOU?

Zit ik voor je?

I WILL LEAVE IT BY THIS

Ik wil het hierbij laten

3

THE MEETING
STARTS

Once the meeting starts, the chairman hates them all heartely welcome and gives the word to the first speaker. They deal out the staple or read the subject hard up before them.

I HATE YOU ALL HEARTILY WELCOME

Ik heet u allen hartelijk welkom

I WISH YOU A PLEASANT PERIOD

Ik wens u een prettige tijd

DO WE NEED A SANDWALKER?

Hebben we een zandloper nodig?

WE WILL GO OVER TO THE ORDER OF THE DAY

We gaan over tot de orde van de dag

WHOME MAY I GIVE THE WORD?

Wie mag ik het woord geven?

I WOULD LIKE TO HAND OVER THE MEETING TO THE FIRST SPEAKER

Ik zou graag het woord willen geven aan de eerste spreker

BUCK!

Bukken!

AM I SITTING IN YOUR LIGHT?

Zit ik in uw licht?

COULD YOU PLEASE DEAL OUT THE STAPLE?

Zou u alstublieft de stapel kunnen uitdelen?

... OR SHALL I READ IT HARD UP BEFORE YOU?

... of zal ik het hardop voorlezen?

I HAVE A LONG WASHING LIST

Ik heb een lange waslijst

WHEN DID YOU SEND IT, AS THERE WAS NO MAIL IN THE BUS?

Wanneer heeft u het gestuurd, want er was geen post in de bus?

I ALREADY SENT IT SOMEWHERE HALF 2004!

Ik heb het al ergens halverwege 2004 verstuurd!

I HAVE BITTEN MYSELF FAST IN THIS SUBJECT

Ik heb me vastgebeten in dit onderwerp

WE BACK YOU TO HELP US

We smeken je ons te helpen

IT WILL WHAT SAY

Het wil wat zeggen

I DO NOT WANT TO FALL WITH THE DOOR IN HOUSE

Ik wil niet met de deur in huis vallen

THIS IS GOING MUCH FURTHER THAN WHAT YOU SAID

Dit gaat veel verder dan wat je zei

I DON'T WILL GO INTO THIS!

Ik ga hier niet op in!

I DO NOT WANT TO MOW AWAY THE GRASS FOR YOUR FEET

Ik wil het gras niet voor je voeten wegmaaien

I DO NOT BELIEVE THAT YOU CAN GET IT FROM THE GROUND

Ik geloof niet dat je het van de grond kunt krijgen

HOW WELL, HAVING THAT SAID, THE MEETING IS NOT FOR NOTHING

Hoewel, dat gezegd hebbende, is de vergadering niet voor niets

4

GENERAL
STATEMENTS

Now general statements are being
made. That somebody has not fallen
on his behind head, that another
does not do this for nothing and
that this is very short through the
curve. But, although this is not to
do, they try to get the noses in the
same direction.

I PREPARED SOMETHING WITH WHICH YOU ARE GOING TO WORK WITH

Ik heb iets voorbereid waarmee jullie gaan werken

I WOULD DO IT AGAINST ALL PRICE

Ik zou het tegen elke prijs doen

YOU CAN HAVE IT AS YOU WANT

Je kunt het zo krijgen als je wilt

WHAT WE SEE MORE AND MORE OVERALL IN EUROPE

Wat we meer en meer zien overal in Europa

ANYWHERE NEAR IN THE FUTURE THIS WILL DISAPPEAR AS SNOW FOR THE SUN

Ergens in de nabije toekomst verdwijnt dit als sneeuw voor de zon

WE SHOULD STOP COFFEE THICK LOOKING

We moeten ophouden met koffiedik kijken

I HAVE NOT FALLEN ON MY BEHIND HEAD!

Ik ben niet op m'n achterhoofd gevallen!

THERE IS NOTHING ON THE HAND

Er is niets aan de hand

I DON'T DO THIS FOR NOTHING

Ik doe dit niet voor niets

AS HE NEEDS A BIG LOANING, HE HAS CHANGED FROM BANK

Aangezien hij een grote lening nodig heeft, is hij van bank veranderd

WITH THAT ALL THAT DOES NOT PLAY

Met dat al speelt dat niet

SHALL WE RUN IT THROUGH?

Zullen we erdoorheen lopen?

IT IS RUNNING OUT OF HAND

Het loopt uit de hand

WE SHOULD STOP NAVEL STARING

We moeten ermee ophouden naar onze navel te staren

I DISTENTIATE MYSELF FROM THIS

Ik distantieer me hiervan

YOU ARE STICKING YOUR HEAD IN THE SAND

Je steekt je hoofd in 't zand

DON'T BREAK ME THE BACK OPEN

Breek me de bek niet open

IT WILL TAKE SOME TIME TO COME OF THE GROUND

Het duurt even voordat het van de grond komt

THAT IS VERY SHORT THROUGH THE CURVE

Dat is erg kort door de bocht

HE STOOD WITH MOUTH OPEN

Hij stond met open mond

IT IS NOT A ONE DAY FLY

Het is niet een eendagsvlieg

LET'S PARALIZE THIS

We moeten dit parallel laten lopen

WHAT FOR EXAMPLE CAN YOU GIVE?

Wat voor voorbeeld kunt u geven?

JUST SAY IT OUT OF YOUR HEAD

Zeg het maar uit je hoofd

THIS IS THE MOST INTERESTING VIRGIN

Dit is de meest interessante versie

HE HAD OTHER FIGURES IN HIS HEAD

Hij had andere cijfers in z'n hoofd

I HAD IT A LITTLE BIT DIFFICULT

Ik had het een beetje moeilijk

WE HAVE TO THIN IT OUT

We moeten het uitdunnen

THIS WRINKLES A BELL

Er rinkelt een bel

THIS IS NOT TO DO

Dit is niet te doen

WE SHOULD GET THE NOSES IN THE SAME DIRECTION

We moeten de neuzen in dezelfde richting krijgen

5

THE MEETING IS
PROGRESSING

Whilst the meeting progresses, people ask if it can or if it not can. As there is a lot of wet finger work, everyone has to look further than their nose is long. If they are on glad ice, this is all madness on a small stick.

WHICH TALKING POINTS DO WE STILL HAVE?

Welke gesprekspunten hebben we nog?

WHAT FOR MONEY ARE WE TALKING ABOUT?

Over hoeveel geld hebben we het eigenlijk?

I ALSO DO NOT KNOW WHAT IT BRINGS UP

Ik weet ook niet wat het opbrengt

CAN IT OR CAN IT NOT?

Kan het of kan het niet?

THIS IS SOMETHING I HAVE SOMETHING TO DO WITH

Hier heb ik iets mee te maken

YOU SHOULD BE FACTURING MUCH EARLIER

Je moet veel eerder factureren

AS I SAID YOU, THIS IS WET FINGER WORK

Zoals ik je vertelde, is dit nattevingerwerk

WE HAVE TO LOOK FURTHER THAN OUR NOSE IS LONG

We moeten verder kijken dan onze neus lang is

I WILL EXPLAIN YOU LATER

Ik zal 't je later uitleggen

YOU CAN STOP THIS IN MY BOX

U kunt dit in mijn doos stoppen

I DON'T WANT TO SHOOT MY HERBS

Ik wil m'n kruit niet verschieten

YOU ARE ALREADY A LITTLE ON ROAD

Je bent al een beetje op weg

YOU ARE ON GLAD ICE!

Je bent op glad ijs!

I WANT TO CONVERSATE PRIVATELY WITH YOU

Ik zou graag apart met u willen praten

HOW LATE IS IT?

Hoe laat is het?

WE SHOULD KEEP AN EYE ON THE TIME

We moeten een oog op de tijd houden

KEEP IT IN THE WHOLES

Houd 't in de gaten

THAT'S HOW THAT GOES

Zo gaat dat

WHAT YOU GOT OVER?

Hoeveel heb je overgehouden?

THERE ARE VARIOUS FORCEFIELDS

Er zijn diverse krachtenvelden

THE BELTS THAT I HAVE TO ROW WITH

De riemen waarmee ik moet roeien

HE RELATIVATES QUITE A LOT

Hij relativeert nogal

IT QUICKLY PETERED OUT

Het pieterde snel uit

IT LOOKS HERE LIKE A PLAY GARDEN

Het lijkt hier wel een speeltuin

WE ARE NOT MORE INTERESTED

We zijn niet meer geïnteresseerd

CONTRARIOUS TO WHAT YOU SAID BEFORE, THE ARGUMENTS ARE FOR THE PICKING-UP

In tegenstelling tot wat u net zei, liggen de argumenten voor het oprapen

ALL MADNESS ON A SMALL STICK

Alle gekheid op een stokkie

6

THINGS ARE NOT GOING WELL

Once things are not going well,
some cannot hold it longer out.
They nearly go over their neck as
they are the child of the bill. While
they are sitting with their mouth full
of teeth, it is not very hopegiving.

SOMEBODY IS SAWING ON MY CHAIRPOTES

Iemand zaagt aan m'n poten

YOU HAVE BEEN FOPPED!

Je bent gefopt!

I CANNOT HOLD IT LONGER OUT

Ik kan het niet langer uithouden

I NEARLY WENT OVER MY NECK

Ik ging bijna over m'n nek

SO CAN IT NOT LONGER

Zo kan het niet langer

SAY SOMETHING!

Zeg iets!

FALL DEAD!

Val dood!

I KNOW FROM NOTHING

Ik weet van niets

FORGET IT BUT!

Vergeet het maar!

DON'T UNDERSTAND ME WRONG

Begrijp me niet verkeerd

THE MEETING IS WALKING OUT

De vergadering loopt uit

WE HAVE THE WIND AGAINST US

We hebben de wind tegen

THAT SAYS NOTHING!

Dat zegt niets!

IT DOES NOT HAVE SIN TO DO THAT

Het heeft geen zin om dat te doen

WHY DON'T YOU GO GEESEBOARDING?

Waarom ga je niet ganzeborden?

THEY TRY TO GET AWAY FROM UNDER

Ze proberen eronderuit te komen

IN GREAT LINES I AGREE

In grote lijnen ben ik het eens

WE ARE FACING WITH A DISASTER

We worden geconfronteerd met een ramp

I SAT WITH MY MOUTH FULL OF TEETH

Ik zat met m'n bek vol tanden

HE WAS LICKING HIS WOUNDS

Hij likte z'n wonden

THIS IS NOT VERY HOPEGIVING

Dit is niet erg hoopgevend

LET IT WALK!

Laat maar lopen!

THIS IS UNOVERCOMEABLE

Dit is onoverkoombaar

HE IS TOTALLY IN THE WAR

Hij is totaal in de war

HE SHOULD BE DISMISSED ON STANDING FOOT

Hij moet op staande voet worden ontslagen

YOU SHOULD NOT TRY TO GET AWAY FROM UNDER

Je moet niet proberen eronderuit te komen

THIS IS NOT TO DO

Dit is niet te doen

IT IS ME WHAT!

Het is me wat!

DO WHAT!

Doe wat!

WE ARE THE CHILD OF THE BILL

We zijn het kind van de rekening

THEY DO NOT PICK IT

Ze pikken het niet

WE LEAVE IT GO

We laten het gaan

WE DO NOT GET OUT

We komen er niet uit

IT IS ALL FIREWOOD

Het is allemaal brandhout

WE ARE WALKING BEHIND

We lopen achter

I WOULD LIKE TO LEAVE IT HERE

Ik zou het hierbij willen laten

FAST WAY!

Snel weg!

7

TIME-OUT

During the time-out they have a little under us. As it is not round yet it has to be checked point for point. They must put water in the wine. If they go through like this, there will be no signage of the contract.

I AM COMPLETELY CHEWED OUT

Ik ben volledig uitgekauwd

WHAT YOU SAY

Wat je zegt

CAN WE HAVE A LITTLE UNDER US?

Kunnen we een onderonsje hebben?

YES, LET'S SHARE THIS ONLY WITH US FOUR

Ja, laten we dit slechts met z'n vieren delen

WE PAY THROUGH OUR NOSE

We betalen door onze neus

INDEED, THIS IS NOT FOR THE PUSSY

Dit is inderdaad niet voor de poes

I'M GOING TO BUY IT ALL UP

Ik ga het allemaal opkopen

HE IS IN HIS ELEMENT

Hij is in z'n element

WE HAVE TO SHRAP ARTICLE 12

We moeten artikel 12 schrappen

WHAT YOU?

Wat jij?

WE HAVE TO CUT KNOTS

We moeten knopen doorhakken

YOU SHOULD WORK HIM IN

Je moet hem inwerken

DO YOU GET OUT OF IT?

Kom je eruit?

WE NEED TO HOLD SOMETHING BEHIND THE HAND

We moeten iets achter de hand houden

HE HAS BEEN SADDLED UP WITH THE ISSUE

Hij is met het probleem opgezadeld

IT IS NOT ROUND YET

Het is nog niet rond

I WORK MYSELF THE BLUBBERS

Ik werk me de blubbers

YOU ARE VERY HEAVY ON THE HAND

Je bent erg zwaar op de hand

BUT HE IS UNSPORTY

Maar hij is onsportief

YOU SHOULD PLAY AN ACTIVER ROLE!

Je moet een actievere rol spelen!

THAT GIVES YOU TO THINK

Dat geeft je te denken

I GIVE MY VOICE TO PETER

Ik geef mijn stem aan Peter

THROUGH THE BANK TAKEN I AGREE WITH YOU

Door de bank genomen ben ik 't met je eens

I DID IT WITH A CLOPPING HEART

Ik deed het met een kloppend hart

WE HAVE AGAIN TO CHECK IT POINT FOR POINT

We moeten het weer punt voor punt nakijken

OK, LET'S TAKE IT THROUGH ONE MORE TIME

Goed, laten we het nog een keer nakijken

WE ROAM IT OFF

We romen het af

WE MUST PUT WATER IN THE WINE

We moeten water bij de wijn doen

IF WE GO THROUGH LIKE THIS, THERE WILL BE NO SIGNAGE OF THE CONTRACT

Als we zo doorgaan, wordt het contract niet getekend

8

THINGS ARE
GOING WELL

Now that things go well, everyone is hanging on his lips. They are not anymore on glad ice, as they have found the egg of Columbus. Nobody can prick through it. We fell with our nose in the butter.

WE ARE A WHOLE END!

We zijn een heel end!

WE WERE HANGING ON YOUR LIPS

We hingen aan je lippen

IT IS VERY HOPE GIVING

Het is zeer hoopgevend

YOU LOOK LIKE TWO HANDS ON ONE BELLY

Jullie lijken wel twee handen op een buik

I ALWAYS GET MY SIN

Ik krijg altijd m'n zin

GOOD SO!

Goed zo!

ARE WE NOT ON GLAD ICE?

Zijn we niet op glad ijs?

SOMETHING HANGS ABOVE OUR HEAD

Er hangt ons iets boven 't hoofd

NO, WE ARE BACK ON THE HORSE

Nee, we zijn weer op 't paard

I WANT TO HIGHER THE RETURN

Ik wil het resultaat verbeteren

THAT'S THE EGG OF COLUMBUS

Dat is het ei van Columbus

I SEE A SMALL LIGHT POINT

Ik zie een lichtpuntje

THEY WILL SOON WALK IN THE RED FIGURES

Ze zullen spoedig in de rode cijfers lopen

HE DID NOT PRICK THROUGH IT

Hij prikte er niet doorheen

THAT CAN WELL

Dat kan wel

OLD COOK!

Oude koek!

I HAD IT TOTALLY MISS

Ik had het totaal mis

WHAT NICE!

Wat leuk!

HE IS THE CIGAR

Hij is de sigaar

IT HAS A HIGH EFFECTIVITY

Het heeft een hoge effectiviteit

SO IS IT!

Zo is het!

I FOLLOW YOU ON THE FOOT

Ik volg je op de voet

I WILL KEEP A FINGER ON THE POLES

Ik houd een vinger aan de pols

HE FELL WITH HIS NOSE IN THE BUTTER

Hij viel met z'n neus in de boter

IT IS ON THE PLANK

Het ligt op de plank

GO YOUR GANG!

Ga je gang!

9

AGREEMENT AND SIGNAGE OF CONTRACT

Agreement has been reached on the whole rim ram. They will go in sea with each other. It was not for nothing. The document still needs some refinery, but then the chairman signs on his backside and lifts the meeting.

WE GO IN SEA WITH YOU

We gaan met jullie in zee

BUT WE NEED THIS IN WRITE

Maar we willen dit op papier hebben

WE APPRECIATE THE CONFIDENCE THAT YOU HAVE OUTSPOKEN

We appreciëren het vertrouwen dat u heeft uitgesproken

YOU HAVE BEEN VERY HELPY

U bent erg hulpvaardig geweest

WE ARE ON THE ROAD ACHIEVING OUR TARGETS

We zijn op weg om onze doelstellingen te bereiken

YOU WERE SITTING GOOD IN YOUR SKIN

Je zat goed in je vel

IT STILL NEEDS A REFINERY HERE AND THERE

Het moet hier en daar nog wat verfijnd worden

WE HAVE DISCUSSED THIS UNDER EACH OTHER

We hebben dit onder elkaar besproken

THIS MAKES PART OF A GREATER PLAN

Dit maakt onderdeel uit van een groter plan

THIS IS AN INTERESTING CONSTATATION

Dit is een interessante constatering

LET US MAKE THE DOCUMENT OFF

Laten we het document afmaken

IT LUCKS WELL

Het lukt wel

WE CAME OVER IT

We zijn eroverheen gekomen

IT IS FINALLY SO FAR

Het is eindelijk zover

I DOCTORED IT OUT

Ik heb het uitgedokterd

THEY HAVE IT ALL

Ze hebben het al

IT WAS NOT FOR NOTHING

Het was niet voor niets

I TAKE OFF MY PET

Ik neem m'n pet af

ALL WITH ALL WE AGREE WITH THE WHOLE RIM RAM

Al met al zijn we het met de hele rimram eens

THE SIGNAGE OF THE CONTRACT IS THE HIGH POINT OF THE MEETING

Het tekenen van het contract is het hoogtepunt van de vergadering

COULD YOU SIGN ON MY BACKSIDE?

Kunt u op de achterkant van mijn kopie tekenen?

WE ARE NEARING THE END OF THE MEETING

We naderen het einde van de vergadering

THE CHAIRMAN LIFTED THE MEETING

De voorzitter hief de vergadering op

10

FAREWELL DINNER

The farewell dinner starts. The ceremony master invites the guests to come on table. They eat slip soles. The wine is over the hill. The feast programme is coming to an end. The chairman thanks them from the bottom of his heart and from his wife's bottom.

WE HAVE PREPARED A FEAST PROGRAMME

We hebben een feestprogramma voorbereid

HE IS THE CEREMONY MASTER

Hij is de ceremoniemeester

HE INVITES THEM TO COME ON TABLE: 'ON TABLE!'

Hij vraagt ze aan tafel te gaan: 'Aan tafel!'

THE JAPANESE ALWAYS INVITE YOU, THE DUTCH ARE NOT SO HOSPITAL

De Japanners nodigen je altijd uit,

Nederlanders zijn niet zo gastvrij

I RECOMMEND SLIP SOLES

Ik beveel sliptongetjes aan

IT IS GOOD FOR THE LINE

Het is goed voor de lijn

WOULD YOU LIKE WINE OR A FRESH DRINK?

Wilt u wijn of een frisdrank?

DO THESE BOTTLES HAVE STATION MONEY?

Hebben deze flessen statiegeld?

THE BOTTLE HAS A BAD CLOSAL

De fles heeft een slechte sluiting

THE KEEPABILITY IS LIMITED

De houdbaarheid is beperkt

THE WINE IS OVER THE HILL

De wijn is niet meer goed

THE WINE IS UP!

De wijn is op!

COULD I HAVE SOME TOAST, OR DO YOU NOT HAVE A BREAD ROOSTER?

Mag ik wat toast, of heeft u geen broodrooster?

A TOAST? YES, I SPEAK OUT A TOAST ON MR. RIJKENS

Een toast? Ja, ik toast op de heer Rijkens

IT SPEAKS VOLUMES

Het spreekt boekdelen

WE ARE MAKING IT GOOD BY A CONTRIBUTION TO YOUR SPARE POT

We maken het goed door een bijdrage aan je spaarpot

A COLLECTION WILL BE HELD FOR A NEW CARPET. ALL THOSE WISHING TO DO SOMETHING ON THE NEW CARPET ARE ASKED TO DO SO

Er zal een collecte worden gehouden voor een nieuw kleed. Eenieder die eraan mee wenst te doen, wordt gevraagd dat te doen

OK, STOP IT THERE IN

Goed, stop het er maar in

HE HAS ONE OVER

Hij heeft er een over

YOU SHOULD NEVER LOOK A GIVEN HORSE IN THE BACK

Je mag een gegeven paard nooit in de bek kijken

I DO NOT LIKE HOUSE ANIMALS

Ik hou niet van huisdieren

IT TASTES FOR MORE

Het smaakt naar meer

YOU ARE AN EXCELLENT UNDERTAKER

Je bent een uitstekende ondernemer

HE IS TAKING THE MIDDLE NIGHT FLIGHT

Hij neemt de vlucht middernacht

I WILL TRAVEL WITH ONLY ONE COFFER

Ik reis maar met één koffer

PLEASE CALL ME UP WHEN YOU ARE IN HOLLAND

Bel me als je in Nederland bent

I WILL JOT IT DOWN ON MY BLOCNOTE

Ik schrijf het op m'n blocnote

HOPELY YOU ENJOYED IT

Hopelijk vond je het gezellig

THIS WAS A LOVELY FAREWELL FEAST

Dit was een heerlijk afscheidsfeest

REALLY, DO COME AND SEARCH US UP!

Kom ons echt eens opzoeken!

MAY I THANK YOUR COCK FOR THE LOVELY DINNER?

Mag ik uw kok bedanken voor het heerlijke diner?

I THANK YOU FROM THE BOTTOM OF MY HEART AND ALSO FROM MY WIFE'S BOTTOM

Ik bedank u hartelijk mede namens mijn vrouw

TILL SOON!

Tot spoedig!

'THE CHAOS', OR 'A DUTCHMAN'S DIFFICULTIES WITH THE ENGLISH LANGUAGE', BY DR. GERARD NOLST TRENITÉ (1870-1946)

Dearest creature in Creation,

Studying English pronunciation,

I will teach you in my verse

Sounds like corpse, corps, horse and worse,

It will keep you, Susy, busy,

Make your head with heat grow dizzy;

Tear in eye your dress you'll tear,

So shall I! Oh, hear my prayer,

Pray, console your loving poet,

Make my coat look new, dear, sew it!

Just compare heart, beard and heard,

Dies and diet, lord and word,

Sword and sward, retain and Britain,

(Mind the latter, how it's written);

Made has not the sound of bade;

Say-said, pay-paid, laid, but plaid.

Now I surely will not plague you

With such words as vague and ague,

But be careful how you speak,

Say, gush, bush and break and bleak,

Previous, precious; fuchsia, via;

Pipe, snipe, recipe and choir,

Cloven, oven; how and low;

Script, receipt; shoe, poem, toe.

Hear me say, devoid of trickery:

Daughter, laughter and Terpsichore,

Typhoid; measles, topsails, aisles;

Exiles, similes, reviles;

Wholly, holly; signal, signing;

Thames; examining, combining;

Real, zeal, mauve, gauze and gauge,

Marriage, foliage, mirage, age.

Query does not rhyme with very,

Nor does fury sound like bury.

Host, lost, post and doth, cloth, loth,

Job, Job, blossom, bosom, oath.

My oppugnant, keen oppugners,

Bowing-bowing, banjo-tuners,

In their yachts or their canoes;

Puisne, truism; use, to use.

Though the difference seems little,

We say actual, but victual.

Seat, sweat; chaste, castle; leigh, eight, height;

Put, nut, granite and unite.

Reefer does not rhyme with 'deafer',

Feoffer does, and zephyr, heifer.

Dull, bull, Geoffrey, George; ate, late;

Hint, pint; senate, sedate;

Scenic, Arabic, pacific;

Science, conscience; scientific,

Tour, but our and succour, four;

Gas, alas, and Arkansas!

Sea, idea, guinea, area,

Psalm; Maria, but malaria;

Youth, south, southern; cleanse and clean;

Doctrine, turpentine, marine.

Compare alien with Italian,

Dandelion with battalion,

Mark the difference, moreover,

Between mover, plover, Dover,

Leeches, breeches; wise, precise;

Chalice but police and lice.

Camel; constable, unstable;

Principle, disciple; label;

Petal, penal and canal;

Wait, surmise, plait, promise; pal,

Suit, suite, ruin, circuit, conduit

Rhyme with 'shirk it' and 'beyond it',

But it is not hard to tell,

Why it's pall, mall, but Pall Mall.

Muscle, muscular; gaol; iron;

Timber, climber; bullion, lion.

Worm and storm; chaise, chaos, chair;

Senator, spectator, mayor.

Ivy, privy; famous. Clamour

And enamour rhyme with 'hammer',

Pussy, hussy and possess,

Desert, but dessert, address.

Golf, wolf; countenance, lieutenants

Hoist, in lieu of flags, left pennants.

River, rival; tomb, bomb, comb;

Doll and roll and some and home.

Stranger does not rhyme with anger,

Neither does devour with clangour.

Soul, but foul and gaunt, but aunt;

Font, front, wont; want, grand and grant.

Shoes, goes, does. Now first say: finger;

Then say: singer, ginger, linger.

Scholar, vicar and cigar,

Solar, mica, war and far.

From 'desire': desirable – admirable from

'admire';

Lumber, plumber; bier, but brier.

Chatham, brougham; renown but known,

Knowledge; done, but gone and tone,

One, anemone; Balmoral;

Kitchen, lichen; laundry, laurel,

Gertrude, German; wind and mind;

Scene, Melpomene; mankind;

Tortoise; turquoise, chamois-leather,

Reading, Reading, heathen, heather.

This phonetic labyrinth

Gives moss, Gross, brook, broach, ninth, plinth.

Billet does not end like ballet;

Bouquet, wallet, mallet, chalet.

Blood and flood are not like food,

Nor is mould like should and would.

Banquet is not like parquet,

Which exactly rhymes with khaki.

Discount, viscount, load and broad;

Toward, to forward, to reward.

Ricocheted and croqueting, croquet?

Right! Your pronunciation is O.K.

Rounded, wounded; grieve and sieve;

Friend and fiend; alive and live;

Liberty, library; heave and heaven;

Rachel, ache, moustache; eleven.

We say hallowed, but allowed;

People, leopard; towed but vowed.

Sally with ally; yea, ye,

Eye, I, ay, aye, whey, key, quay!

Say aver, but ever, fever,

Neither, leisure, skein, receiver.

Never guess, it's not safe:

We say calves, valves, half, but Ralph!

Heron; granary, canary,

Crevice and device, and eyrie,

Face, but preface, but grimace,

Phlegm, phlegmatic, ass, glass, bass-

Bass; large, target, gin, give, verging;

Ought, out, joust and scour, but scourging;

Ear, but earn; and wear and tear

Do not rhyme with 'here', but 'ere'.

Seven is right, but so is even;

Hyphen, roughen, nephew, Stephen;

Monkey, donkey, clerk and jerk;

Asp, grasp, wasp, demesne; cork, work.

Pronunciation – think of psyche!

Is a paling, stout and spikey;

Won't it make you lose your wits,

Writing 'groats' and saying groats?

It's a dark abyss or tunnel,

Strewn with stones, like rowlock, gunwhale,

Islington and Isle of Wight,

Housewife, verdict, and indict!

Don't you think so reader, rather,

Saying lather, bather, father?

Finally: which rhymes with 'enough':

Though, through, plough, cough, hough or

tough?

Hiccough has the sound of 'cup'...

My advice is: GIVE IT UP!

PROPOSAL
FOR A MORE
USER-FRIENDLY
ENGLISH

Recently I became aware of a proposal to the Council of Ministers of the European Union for the phased introduction of a Pan-European standard for a more user-friendly communication:

Quote

'Having chosen English as the preferred language in the European Union, the European Parliament has commissioned a feasibility study into ways of improving efficiency in communications between Government Departments.

European officials have often pointed out that English spelling is unnecessarily difficult. For example: cough, plough, rough, through and thorough. What is clearly needed is a phased programme of changes to iron out these anomalies. The programme would, of course, be administered by a committee staffed at top level by all participating nations.

In the first year, for example, the committee would suggest using 's' instead of the soft 'c'. Sertainly, sivil servants in all sities would reseive this news with joy. Then the hard 'c' kould be replaced by a 'k', sinse both letters are pronounsed alike. Not only would this klear up konfusion in the minds of klerikal workers, but keyboards kould be made with fewer letters.

There would be growing enthousiasm when in the sekond year it was announsed that the troublesome 'ph' would hensforth be written with 'f'. This would make words like 'fotograf' twenty persent shorter in print.

In the third year, publik akseptanse of the new spelling kould be ekspekted to reash the stage where more komplikated shanges are possible. Governments would enkourage the removal of double letters, which have always been a deterent to akurate speling.

We would al agre that the horible mes of silent 'e's in the languag is disgrasful. Therefor, we kould drop thes and kontinu to read and writ as though nothing had hapend. By this tim it would be four years sins the skem began and peopl would be reseptiv to steps sutsh as replasing 'th' by 'z'. Perhaps zen ze funktion of 'w' kould be taken on by ze 'v', vitsh is, afteral, half a 'w'. Shortly after zis, ze unesesary 'o' kuld be dropd from vords kontaining 'ou'. Similar arguments vud ofkors be aplid to ozer kombinatons of leters.

Kontinuing zis proses yer after yer, ve vud eventuli hav a reli sensibl vriten styl. After tventi yers zer vud be no mor trubls, difikultis and evrivun vud find it ezi to understand ech ozer.

Zen ze drems of ze Guvenmnt vud finali hav

kum tru!!!'

Unquote

AFTERWORD

In dit nawoord wil ik even ingaan op het slechte
taalgebruik van de Nederlander.
Bijna elke Nederlander spreekt wel enigszins
Engels en kan zich behelpen in de Engelse taal:
'How do you do and how do you do your
wife?' Buitenlanders zijn daar snel van
gecharmeerd.

Maar het wordt geheel anders als de taal er
tijdens onderhandelingen echt op aankomt en
als er uit hetgeen de Engelsman zegt door
Nederlanders conclusies worden getrokken. In
mijn werkzame leven heb ik dat vaak
meegemaakt. Zo meldde ik weleens dat een
bepaalde partner een bepaald onderwerp niet
zag zitten. Als bazen daar dan aan twijfelden,

stuurden ze er graag iemand op af om

poolshoogte te nemen. Als hij dan terugkwam

zei hij weleens: 'Rijkens zit er helemaal naast.

Ze vinden het onderwerp "interesting" en ze

hebben toegezegd: "We will look into it, we

will study the subject".'

In werkelijkheid is voor Engelsen de kreet

'interesting' de grootste dooddoener die er

bestaat en betekent het: 'Dat nooit!' 'We will

look into it' is een nette manier om te zeggen:

'Vergeet het maar!' 'Not bad' daarentegen

betekent: 'That's good, very good!'

Het bijgaande lijstje omschrijft het onderwerp

heel aardig:

What the English say	**What the English mean**
(Very) interesting	I do not agree at all I do not believe you
I hear what you say	I disagree and do not want to discuss it any further
With the greatest respect...	I think you are wrong (or a fool)
(That's) not bad	That's good or very good
O, by the way.../Incidentally...	The primary purpose of our discussion is
Quite good	A bit disappointing
Perhaps you would like to think about it	Do it, or be prepared to justify yourself
I was a bit disappointed that.../It is a pity you...	I am most upset and cross
Could we consider some other options?	I don't like your idea
I'll bear it in mind	I will do nothing about it
I will think about it	It's a bad idea, I will most definitely not do it
I'm sure it's my fault	It is your fault!
That is an original point of view	You must be crazy!
You'll get there eventually	You don't stand a chance in hell
I almost agree	I don't agree at all
We will look into it, we will study the subject	We will do nothing about it
You must come for dinner sometime	I am not inviting you, just being polite

What the Dutch understand

They are impressed

He accepts my point of view

He is interested in what I have to say

That's not good enough yet

This is not very important

Rather good

Think about the idea, but do what you like

It doesn't really matter

They have not yet decided

They will probably do it

They think it's a good
idea: let's keep developing it

It was their fault

They like my ideas!

Keep on trying, for they agree I'm heading in the right direction

We are not far from agreement

They are interested! They will study the subject

I will get an invitation soon

ABOUT THE
WRITER

Maarten H. Rijkens was born in Amsterdam in 1946. His father being a Unilever director, he lived most of his young years in the outside world and he attended German and British schools. He studied economic science in Rotterdam, the Netherlands, and in St. Gallen, Switzerland. He was a cavalery officer by the hussars of Boreel and spent a year in active service in Germany.

In 1972 he joined Heineken, the international brewers. After having his first period in various marketing positions he started his international career. He worked hardly and came over all in the world for the famous brewer and lived in the USA, Canada, Singapore and Papua New Guinea.

For more than fifteen years he earned his spurs when he was responsible for the Asia Pacific. He was clearly not the first the best. Then, when someone was sawing on his chairpotes, he cut his knots and went with pension in 2004.

With that all, Rijkens is now back on the horse on various supervisory boards and acts in an advisory capacity. He enjoys collecting antiques & art, is interesting in architecture, the preservation of historic buildings, history and genealogy. He is married with Denise and with two children, Claire (22) and Adriaan (18), both studying in the Netherlands, where they all live with much pleasure. There Rijkens is doing well and he is doing his wife well.

Van de bestseller *I always get my sin* zijn al ruim
300.000 exemplaren verkocht. Maar hoe voorkom je
zelf zulke blunders? *We always get our sin too* laat niet
alleen zien welke gekke fouten je in het Engels kunt
maken, maar ook hoe je ze kunt vermijden. Met de vele
nieuwe fouten die Maarten H. Rijkens heeft verzameld is
We always get our sin too een hilarisch vervolg op
I always get my sin en een *must have* voor liefhebbers
van bizar Engels die het zelf wél goed willen doen.